WOMEN OF THE
OLD TESTAMENT

12 STUDIES FOR INDIVIDUALS OR GROUPS

LifeGuide®
BIBLE STUDIES

GLADYS HUNT

IVP Connect

An imprint of InterVarsity Press
Downers Grove, Illinois

InterVarsity Press
P.O. Box 1400, Downers Grove, IL 60515-1426
ivpress.com
email@ivpress.com

InterVarsity Press® *is the book-publishing division of InterVarsity Christian Fellowship/USA*®*, a movement of students and faculty active on campus at hundreds of universities, colleges and schools of nursing in the United States of America, and a member movement of the International Fellowship of Evangelical Students. For information about local and regional activities, visit intervarsity.org.*

LifeGuide® *is a registered trademark of InterVarsity Christian Fellowship.*

All Scripture quotations, unless otherwise indicated, are taken from the Holy Bible, New International Version®. NIV®. Copyright ©1973, 1978, 1984 by International Bible Society. Used by permission of Zondervan Publishing House. All rights reserved.

Cover photograph: © *Mohamad Itani / Trevillion Images*

ISBN 978-0-8308-3064-0

Printed in the United States of America ∞

g green press INITIATIVE *As a member of the Green Press Initiative, InterVarsity Press is committed to protecting the environment and to the responsible use of natural resources. To learn more, visit greenpressinitiative.org.*

P	29	28	27	26	25	
Y	29	28	27	26	25	24

Contents

Getting the Most Out of *Women of the Old Testament*

Why study women of the Old Testament? If that question went through your mind when you first picked up this guide, I can sympathize. I had similar thoughts when I was asked to write it. I hope you will be in for the same pleasant surprise I got when I began to look at the women in this guide more closely. Remote as they may seem, their lives are amazingly relevant.

One of the basic lessons seen in each woman's life is the consistency of cause and effect. Simple faith results in God's care. Living life apart from what you know to be true about God brings disaster. The right action in a crisis exhibits the kind of courage God honors. Believing God against all odds proves his faithfulness. The real stuff of life that makes our character strong or weak is the same today as it was then.

A second observation is that these women had amazing freedom to act. We tend to think that women in the Old Testament lived in a suppressed environment, a patriarchy in which they had few rights. Yet whatever their limitations, they made choices, acted on behalf of others, helped lead people out of bondage, dared to believe God for deliverance, traveled, prayed, took initiative and rescued a whole nation. They were a remarkable lot!

The third observation is that these women, for the most part, were ordinary people. They would not make headlines in any other history book but God's. That's because there are no unimportant people in God's sight. The fact that God recorded their stories for our learning reveals what he considers important.

Some of the choices and decisions these women faced have been replayed again and again in the history of humanity. Satan tried his strategy on the first woman and, finding that it worked, has used it over and over. Basically he got her to doubt whether God had her highest good in mind. Sarah took matters into her own hands because she got tired of waiting for God. Miriam, insecure about her own position, became critical of leadership and paid for it dearly. Do any of their actions remind you of something in your own life?

I chose the women in this guide because there was enough biblical material to allow an inductive study for group discussion. Many others are worthy of your study. Some are described in only a few verses or references, but there is enough material to give an idea of their courage, boldness, decisive action or faith.

As I wrote this guide, I learned many new things that fed my intellectual curiosity—facts about biblical culture, geography and history. The best things I learned, however, came from the inner lives of these women. Their choices challenged me; the lessons they learned had ready application for my life; their faith and praise inspired my own. As you get to know them, I hope you will experience this same enlarging of your spiritual life.

Suggestions for Individual Study

1. As you begin each study, pray that God will speak to you through his Word.

2. Read the introduction to the study and respond to the personal reflection question or exercise. This is designed to help you focus on God and on the theme of the study.

3. Each study deals with a particular passage—so that you can delve into the author's meaning in that context. Read and reread the passage to be studied. If you are studying a book, it will be helpful to read through the entire book prior to the first study. The questions are written using the language of the New International Version, so you may wish to use that version of the Bible. The New Revised Standard Version is also recommended.

4. This is an inductive Bible study, designed to help you discover for yourself what Scripture is saying. The study includes three types of questions. *Observation* questions ask about the basic facts: who, what, when, where and how. *Interpretation* questions delve into the meaning of the passage. *Application* questions help you discover the implications of the text for growing in Christ. These three keys unlock the treasures of Scripture. Write your answers to the questions in the spaces provided or in a personal journal. Writing can bring clarity and deeper understanding of yourself and of God's Word.

5. It might be good to have a Bible dictionary handy. Use it to look up any unfamiliar words, names or places.

6. Use the prayer suggestion to guide you in thanking God for what you have learned and to pray about the applications that have come to mind.

7. You may want to go on to the suggestion under "Now or Later," or you may want to use that idea for your next study.

Suggestions for Members of a Group Study

1. Come to the study prepared. Follow the suggestions for individual study mentioned above. You will find that careful preparation will greatly enrich your time spent in group discussion.

2. Be willing to participate in the discussion. The leader of your group will not be lecturing. Instead, he or she will be encouraging the members of the group to discuss what they have learned. The leader will be asking the questions that are found in this guide.

3. Stick to the topic being discussed. Your answers should be based on the verses which are the focus of the discussion and not on outside authorities such as commentaries or speakers. These studies focus on a particular passage of Scripture. Only rarely should you refer to other portions of the Bible. This allows for everyone to participate in in-depth study on equal ground.

4. Be sensitive to the other members of the group. Listen attentively when they describe what they have learned. You may be surprised by their insights! Each question assumes a variety of answers. Many questions do not have "right" answers, particularly questions that aim at meaning or application. Instead the questions push us to explore the passage more thoroughly.

When possible, link what you say to the comments of others. Also, be affirming whenever you can. This will encourage some of the more hesitant members of the group to participate.

5. Be careful not to dominate the discussion. We are sometimes so eager to express our thoughts that we leave too little opportunity for others to respond. By all means participate! But allow others to also.

6. Expect God to teach you through the passage being discussed and through the other members of the group. Pray that you will have an enjoyable and profitable time together, but also that as a result of the study you will find ways that you can take action individually and/or as a group.

7. Remember that anything said in the group is considered confidential and should not be discussed outside the group unless specific permission is given to do so.

8. If you are the group leader, you will find additional suggestions at the back of the guide.

1

The First Woman

A Far-Reaching Choice

Genesis 3:1-13

The Tempter, described as a crafty serpent, never whispers to us, "Come, I'll teach you to sin." If he tempted us in this way, we would recognize his strategy immediately and declare ourselves. Instead, he comes in disguise, sometimes piously quoting Scripture, carrying on discussions about God or whatever fits his purpose.

GROUP DISCUSSION. How have you experienced the Tempter using your fear of missing out on the good stuff of life to trick you into listening to his lies?

PERSONAL REFLECTION. If someone wanted to entice you to do wrong, what kind of appeal would prove to be the best strategy?

The Tempter knew what the issues were when he approached the first woman. He exploited her not by actions but by his words. He appealed to her desire for the best in life and encouraged her to choose against her understanding of truth. The tragic consequences reveal that no-fault choices are illusions both for Eve and for us. *Read Genesis 3:1-13.*

1. What do you imagine the quality of life was like in the garden

where the first woman lived? Refer briefly to Genesis 2:8-23 to find out the details of "her world."

---

2. The serpent approaches the woman with a discussion about God. What doubts does he raise in her mind regarding God's character (vv. 4-5)?

---

3. Compare the woman's answer to the serpent's question (vv. 1-3) with God's original instruction in 2:17. Why do you think she amplified the instruction?

Have you ever done the same thing? Explain.

---

4. After the serpent departs, what does the woman see when she examines the forbidden tree (v. 6)?

---

5. What was wrong with her focus?

---

6. Do you think the woman knew she was doing wrong when she took the fruit? Why or why not?

7. How does your focus affect your awareness of whether you are yielding to temptation?

___

8. What were the immediate consequences of her action (vv. 7-13)?

___

9. Everything in Eden changed as the result of the woman's choice. Yet what evidence of God's grace do you see (vv. 8-13)?

___

10. It was only one tree and one little piece of fruit. What does Eve's experience teach us about the far-reaching consequences of our choices?

___

11. What strategies help you to thwart the Tempter?

Ask God to sharpen your awareness of his truth and of the Tempter's strategies.

Now or Later

As a personal exercise, recall the hurtful times when the Tempter won in your life (lies, wrong actions, wrong words, wrong attitudes) and what strategy he used. Notice how he preyed on your insecurities, and resolve to resist his wiles.

2

Sarah & Hagar

Waiting for God to Act

Genesis 16; 18:1-15

Do you ever think God needs a little help in keeping his promises? When time passes without answers, the temptation is to take matters into our own hands. It's one thing to believe God answers our prayers and keeps his word; it's another thing to wait for him. Waiting is hard. Believing while waiting is harder still.

GROUP DISCUSSION. Proverbs 13:12 says, "Hope deferred makes the heart sick, but a longing fulfilled is a tree of life." Recall ways in which you have found this proverb to be true in your own life. When is waiting hard, and when is it easy? What does that tell about the human heart?

PERSONAL REFLECTION. How do you react when your prayers go unanswered?

God had made a promise to Abraham and Sarah. He said he would bless the whole world through the child he would give them. At first they waited eagerly. But after years of waiting their faith began to waver. Would God keep his promise? Should they take matters into their own hands? God's timetable is often very different from our own. *Read Genesis 16.*

1. Over a period of two decades God repeated his promise to make a great nation out of Abram's offspring. As the years went by and no child was conceived, how do you think Sarai felt about herself?

2. When Sarai suggested Hagar as a substitute (surrogate) mother, she was following a custom acceptable in her culture. At what point does she regret this decision (16:4-5)?

3. Notice how Sarai blames Abram in verse 5. Why do we want to blame others for our bad decisions?

4. What does Hagar learn about God in her personal struggles over this pregnancy (16:7-14)?

5. Remembering Hagar's position in Abram's household, what would it cost her to obey the angel's instruction?

6. Thirteen years later God again appears to Abram, reminds him of his promise and changes his name to Abraham and Sarai's to Sarah (17:5, 15). *Read Genesis 18:1-15.* To what lengths does God go to demonstrate to Abraham and Sarah the certainty of his promise?

How do you think Abraham and Sarah felt about God after he took these actions?

7. What does the Lord seem to know about Sarah (18:10-15)?

What did Sarah need to learn about the Lord?

8. Is God's knowledge of your private thoughts and fears a comfort or a distress to you? Explain.

9. What choices and possible outcomes face you in times of waiting for God to act on your behalf?

Ask God to teach you what it means to have a truly believing heart that waits for him.

Now or Later

Compare Jeremiah 32:27, Luke 1:37 and Luke 18:27 with Genesis 18:14. Is anything in your life too hard for God?

3

Miriam

A Critical Spirit

Numbers 12

Who hasn't been critical of someone else and said, either aloud or inwardly, "Who does she think she is?" Often we don't understand the details of someone's actions or have all the facts. Our anxiety comes out of our mouths, and we not only hurt ourselves but also sometimes damage the loyalty and well-being of others.

GROUP DISCUSSION. Think about times when you have been critical of another person. As nearly as you can understand yourself, what underlying attitude caused the criticism?

What is the difference between discernment and criticism?

PERSONAL REFLECTION. How do you feel when you are unjustly criticized?

When the children of Israel left Egypt, they had little sense of national identity and were not used to following a leader. Moses' job was not easy. He needed all the support he could get, and the people needed continual reassurance that he was chosen by God to take them to the Promised Land. Sometimes that seemed doubtful in the face of privation and difficulty. Imagine what could have happened to Moses' confidence and to the people when the members of Moses' own family began to criticize his leadership. *Read Numbers 12.*

1. What two criticisms do Miriam and Aaron have about Moses (vv. 1-2)?

2. What do these criticisms imply about Moses' attitude?

How does Miriam and Aaron's view differ from God's evaluation of Moses?

3. How important was Miriam's role in the exodus of the children of Israel from Egypt (see Exodus 2:1-8; 15:20-21 and Micah 6:4)?

4. Miriam and Aaron's attack on their brother may have been provoked by his appointing seventy elders over Israel (Numbers 11:16-17). How might the appointment of elders affect their status and feelings?

5. Explain how you feel when your status or position is threatened. What is your instinctive reaction?

6. How does the Lord respond to the criticisms of Miriam and Aaron (vv. 4-10)?

7. Why do you think God summons all three of them before him?

8. What do we learn about Aaron and Moses from their response to this traumatic event (vv. 10-13)?

9. Why do you think God carried out a seven-day punishment for Miriam (vv. 14-15)?

Why didn't he punish Aaron in the same way?

10. Why is the criticism of spiritual leaders especially dangerous?

11. What is your response to knowing that the Lord hears (v. 2) the criticisms you make against others?

12. After reading this passage, how do you differentiate between offering valid insights into relational situations with a loving spirit and being openly critical?

Ask God to teach you to be more loving.

Now or Later

Check out your personal critical faculties. Do they inspire you to pray or to be negative toward others? What can you do to heighten your awareness of your motives in speaking against others?

4

Rahab

An Unlikely Ally

Joshua 2; 6:15-25

Do you ever feel like you are living in enemy territory? Some people go around hoping no one will suspect they are Christians. It costs to identify yourself with the people of God. It can't be done without genuine faith.

GROUP DISCUSSION. "Faith is being sure of what we hope for and certain of what we do not see." The writer of Hebrews gives this definition of *faith*. What is your definition of *faith?*

What risks are involved in faith?

PERSONAL REFLECTION. Who do you think of as a faith-filled person?

After the death of Moses, God told Joshua to take the land of Canaan from the enemies of God. The major cities of Canaan were in reality small kingdoms, each ruled by a local king. The invasion point was in the plains of Moab on the far side of the Jordan. Joshua sent out a reconnaissance party to check out their first target—the city of Jericho. God had already prepared the heart of one woman in that city who became famous for her good deeds, her faith and her willingness to ally herself with God's people. *Read Joshua 2.*

1. Why do you think the spies chose Rahab's house for lodging?

2. What words would you use to describe Rahab?

3. Why do you think Rahab risked her life for these two men?

4. What risks have you taken to ally yourself with God's people?

5. What did Rahab believe about God (2:9-11)?

How is what we know about God related to taking risks for our faith?

6. How would the agreement Rahab made with the men test her faith?

7. *Read Joshua 6:15-25.* What steps were taken to honor the oath made to Rahab?

How was God's reputation on the line?

8. Read what is said about Rahab in Hebrews 11:31 and James 2:25. Of all the women in the Old Testament, why do you think she is singled out for special comment?

9. Rahab is also mentioned in Matthew 1:5. What were the far-reaching effects of Rahab's decision to ally herself with God's people?

10. What kinds of people can God use to accomplish his purposes?

11. What risks is God calling you to take?

Pray that you will be bolder in taking risks that reveal your faith in God.

Now or Later

Begin to think about practical ways you can take the risk of letting others know of your faith in God and in his Son, Jesus. Be serious enough about this to make a list of specific people or actions that might help you be more open about who you are.

5

Ruth

The Cost of Loyalty

Ruth 1—2

A university student wrote to J. R. R. Tolkien after reading *Lord of the Rings,* "You have made loyalty and courage more meaningful to me."

Loyalty doesn't get much press today. It's present in the lives of many, but it isn't heralded like it used to be when people signed their letters "Your loyal friend."

GROUP DISCUSSION. What does loyalty look like in a person?

What keeps us from being loyal to our family and friends—and even to God?

PERSONAL REFLECTION. How would you define *loyalty?*

The book of Ruth is a simple story about the cost and value of loyalty. It takes place during the period of the judges (c. 1380-1050 B.C.), which were dark and turbulent days for Israel. It provides a glimpse into the lives of ordinary people who show care and loyalty for each other that reflects God's character. *Read Ruth 1.*

---

1. What turbulent circumstances brought Ruth, a Moabite woman, into Naomi's family?

_____

2. What issues did Ruth most likely face in a crosscultural marriage?

_____

3. What are the practical implications of the choice Ruth makes in contrast to the choice Orpah makes?

_____

4. What evidence do you see that Ruth's choice involves more than attachment to Naomi?

_____

5. What choices have you made that are similar to Ruth's?

_____

6. *Read Ruth 2.* Naomi and Ruth arrive in Bethlehem at the time of the barley harvest (1:22). What does Ruth's willingness to be a gleaner tell us about her?

_____

7. How does the regard that Boaz has for Ruth and her position in Israel (2:11-12) differ from Ruth's concept of herself?

8. Put yourself in Ruth's place. How would it feel to be a foreigner, needing to work hard to support your mother-in-law?

9. What do you think motivates Ruth's hard work and her loyalty to Naomi?

What motivates your own loyalty?

10. What loyalties are important to you as a Christian, regardless of cost?

How could you encourage those loyalties?

We tend to think first of ourselves; pray that God will strengthen your own commitment and loyalty to others.

Now or Later

Ruth's story is not all told in this study. The following study, focusing on Naomi, tells the rest of the story. Read Ruth 3 and 4 in preparation for the next discussion.

6

Naomi

Sadness Swallowed Up by Joy

Ruth 3—4

Life is like a grindstone, someone once said, and whether it grinds you down or polishes you depends on the stuff you are made of. It also depends on your view of God. Some people seem to get more hard knocks in life than others, and if you say, "That's not fair," you are probably right. Life isn't always fair. But the question is, even in the hardest circumstances, is God in control? If he is, that means he can change the bitterness of our hard experiences.

GROUP DISCUSSION. What hard experiences are you presently undergoing that you feel are testing what you are made of?

What difference does confidence in God make in handling your pain and disappointment?

PERSONAL REFLECTION. How conscious are you that God is in control of your life? What can you do to feel closer to God?

Naomi is a case study in hardship. During a time of famine, her family became refugees in a foreign land. There she lost her husband, and her two sons also died. Now it seems she has few prospects other than a lonely future. Despite Naomi's trials, Ruth's insistence on returning with her is a strong indication of God's care. Gradually it dawns on Naomi that God has provided for her and Ruth in ways she never expected. In these two chapters we see Naomi's bitterness turned to joy. *Read Ruth 3 and 4.*

1. Naomi's name means "pleasant." When she returns to Bethlehem, why does she suggest a change of name (1:20-21)?

2. A kinsman-redeemer was responsible for protecting the interests of his extended family. What new hope comes to Naomi as a result of Ruth meeting Boaz (2:19-23)?

3. To "spread the corner of your garment over me" (3:9) was a request for marriage. Why might this be a risky plan?

4. What is Naomi's opinion of Boaz's character?

How would you evaluate him from his actions in these two chapters?

5. What is the relationship between your willingness to take risks in your relationship to God and your confidence in his character?

6. What does Naomi gain from the transaction that takes place?

Why does the birth of Obed mean so much to her (4:13-17)?

7. What do you see as the turning point in Naomi's life from the bitterness she expressed as she returned to Bethlehem (1:20) to the joy she feels at the end of the story (4:16)?

8. In what way has God provided a kinsman-redeemer for us?

9. Ruth's son becomes an ancestor of King David. Although Ruth is a Gentile, she is mentioned in the genealogy of Jesus in Matthew 1:5. What do you learn about God from the amazing ways in which he blesses Naomi after all her tragedies?

10. How does this story encourage you personally?

Thank God for the times when he has shown his faithfulness to you and changed your sorrow to joy. Ask him to increase your confidence in his love and care in your life.

Now or Later

Who can you encourage today or tomorrow with your confidence that God knows our disappointments and pain and cares for us?

7

Hannah

From Misery to Praise

1 Samuel 1:1—2:11

Waiting is one of the hardest things we do. So much of life involves waiting, and in an age of instant products, waiting irritates us. But waiting is hardest when we see the clock running on, the years going by, and still our hopes and dreams are unfulfilled.

GROUP DISCUSSION. How do you react—physically, emotionally, spiritually—when years pass by and still your most cherished hopes have not materialized? How have you learned to cope with the tension this brings into your life?

PERSONAL REFLECTION. The Bible speaks often of waiting for the Lord to act and to bless. If we have blessings, how should we act toward those who are still waiting?

Hannah knew about waiting. In a society that measured a woman's worth by her children, Hannah was barren. Year after year she waited in misery for the answer to her prayers. She had two choices: to be bitter or to continue seeking God's help. This study looks at Hannah's journey from misery to praise. *Read 1 Samuel 1.*

1. Why is Hannah's pain so intense (1:2-7)?

2. Hannah turns to God in desperation. What does her prayer reveal about her (1:9-11)?

_____

3. When you are bitter about your disappointments, to whom (or what) do you turn?

What are your expectations?

_____

4. Just as Hannah's response revealed her inner person, what does our response to pain and disappointment reveal about us?

_____

5. How do Hannah's subsequent actions show her certainty that her son was a gift from God?

_____

6. *Read 1 Samuel 2:1-11.* Describe the shift in Hannah's focus between chapters 1 and 2.

What brought this about?

7. What does Hannah believe about God? (Find several strong beliefs.)

_____

8. Which of Hannah's beliefs about God could you state as your own, and how did you come to these beliefs?

_____

9. How would you define what Hannah is doing in verses 1-10?

What is the source of her joy? (Compare it with Hebrews 13:15-16.)

_____

10. What specific things can you learn from Hannah about the solution to the pain of unfulfilled hopes?

What attracts you to Hannah as you look at her character? Ask God to bless you with her faith and joy in worship, with her willingness to give what she most valued to the service of God.

Now or Later

Hannah's song of praise was written down and became part of tradition. Mary's song in Luke 1:46-55 has similarities to Hannah's inspired words. Try writing your own song of praise, telling God what you believe about him.

8

Abigail

A Level-Headed Woman

1 Samuel 25:2-44

How do you act in times of crisis? The easiest way out is to hope that someone else will act! It takes courage to believe that what you do will solve the crisis. It also demands insight into the situation at hand.

GROUP DISCUSSION. How would you define a fool? Can a fool help being a fool?

PERSONAL REFLECTION. Everyone does something foolish at some time or other. How do you handle your foolish mistakes?

The heroine in this study is a woman named Abigail, whose rich husband is a fool. (The biblical story doesn't mince words.) Despite the cultural restrictions on women in her day, Abigail acts courageously and with insight that prevents a massacre. _Read 1 Samuel 25:2-44._

1. As this story begins, what is the life situation of the major characters in the story?

2. From the facts given in the story, do you think David's request of Nabal is reasonable? Why or why not?

3. How does Nabal's information about David differ from that of the servants and Abigail?

4. How do the servants regard Abigail (vv. 14-17)?

5. How does Abigail demonstrate resourcefulness, and what risks does she take (vv. 18-31)?

6. How do you decide when you should be responsible to rescue others from their foolishness?

7. What does Abigail understand about the plan of God in David's life (vv. 28-31)?

8. What phrases and word choices demonstrate Abigail's intelligence and persuasiveness?

9. Who does Abigail rescue by her actions?

10. What ingredients are necessary for courageous action in crisis situations?

11. Think about a crisis that you or someone close to you is facing. What insights do you have about that crisis that could lead to courageous action and rescue for that person?

It's always easier to do nothing. Ask God to give you a discerning heart and mind, and then the courage to act as one of his children who stands for what is right.

Now or Later

Not every idea we have about another person's life or ideas is valid. Write down some guiding principles that can keep you from "trespassing" or "ignoring" issues that come before you.

9

The Shunammite Woman

Taking the Initiative

2 Kings 4:8-37

"I thought he must be a Christian when he took me to his home for dinner and overnight," said a visiting Chinese scholar, recounting how a stranger had offered him hospitality when he was stranded at the airport. Hospitality is a trait repeatedly commended in the Bible. God is hospitable, and he wants his children to be also.

GROUP DISCUSSION. What are the ingredients of hospitality?

What happens when you feel welcomed into someone's life or home?

PERSONAL REFLECTION. Ask yourself: "Am I waiting for certain possessions or a certain lifestyle before exercising hospitality?" What can you do today to show hospitality?

In this story a woman welcomes a "man of God" into her home and is rewarded for doing so—or so it seems until the day her son dies. The initiative she shows in offering hospitality leads her to deeper faith in expecting God to act on her behalf. Her faith and boldness, as well as her generosity, are a model for us. *Read 2 Kings 4:8-37.*

1. How does the Shunammite woman take initiative here?

2. Why did the woman use her resources to help Elisha?

What do you think her generosity meant to Elisha and his servant?

3. Compare your own use of resources. How can you show hospitality even with limited resources?

4. What do you think Elisha's concern for her needs (vv. 12-14) meant to the Shunammite woman?

Why do you think the woman didn't initiate her own request to Elisha (v. 14)?

5. After being given a son and raising him to boyhood, the woman now faces a terrible loss (vv. 18-20). How does she respond to the death of her son (vv. 21-30)?

6. How do you account for the implied accusation the woman makes against Elisha (v. 28)?

7. When have you spoken accusing words like these to God or to others?

_____

8. What is the woman's strong resolve in the face of her son's death?

What alternative action might she have chosen?

_____

9. When you feel distressed about something in your life, how do you react?

_____

10. How can we develop a foundation of faith and trust in God before times of crisis come to us?

Ask God to help you to always turn to him as the source of both goodness and power to meet your needs.

Now or Later

We meet the Shunammite woman again in 2 Kings 8:1-6 when she verifies the ministry of Elisha. Like the woman, what can you tell about the wonderful works of God on your behalf? Be specific.

10

Esther

Captive in a Strange Land

Esther 2—4

The emotional effects of dysfunctional family life in today's society are commonly discussed in books and on talk shows. Many people have to cope with disadvantaged beginnings. It is a significant problem, especially for people who are caught in such circumstances. But for a culture as psychologized as ours, it can become the excuse for poor behavior. We can choose to be victims of our circumstances.

GROUP DISCUSSION. As you look over your life, what factors are outside of your control?

What are you most sorry about, or what makes you the most angry?

How do you keep from letting your disadvantages limit you as a person?

PERSONAL REFLECTION. Look at your attitude toward life and consider whether you are dwelling on the negatives instead of overcoming your difficulties.

Esther is certainly a disadvantaged young woman. But she is a woman with inner strength. She does more than cope. We have no idea how many tears she shed, but she rises to make the most of the circumstances in which she finds herself. *Read Esther 2—3*.

1. What factors in Esther's life are outside of her control?

2. What could she control?

3. Reread questions 1 and 2, putting your name in place of Esther's. How relevant are these questions in your life?

4. Describe the situation of the women who are chosen (2:2-4, 12-14).

5. What details of the story give you insight into Mordecai's character?

6. *Read Esther 4.* How did Mordecai handle this outrage against the Jews (4:1-4, 7-8, 12-14, 17)?

7. What philosophical/theological understanding undergirds the request Mordecai makes of Esther?

8. What three arguments does he use to persuade Esther to act (4:13-14)?

9. When threatening circumstances arise, what makes it difficult to believe that God is at work behind the scenes?

———————————————————————————

10. How is Esther's reply (4:15-16) a confession of faith, even though she does not mention God?

———————————————————————————

11. Looking back over this part of the story, in what ways does Esther overcome her circumstances?

———————————————————————————

12. What do you do when circumstances hem you in?

What are your options?

Ask God to help you see clearly what circumstances in your past need to be overcome because they are limiting your freedom to be all that God wants you to be.

Now or Later

Record all the evidence you can muster that assures you that your life is safe in God's hands. Like Mordecai, are you certain that life is not just a collection of random events but rather that it is controlled by God?

11

Esther

Courage to Act

Esther 5:1-8; 7—8

All the great stories of history are about virtues like loyalty, honor or courage fleshed out in someone's life circumstances. We need to see how these virtues look in a fellow human being so we can choose them for our own lives. Then we realize that fear can be laid aside and the right action taken, even though the outcome is uncertain.

GROUP DISCUSSION. What is courage? Do you need it only in times of danger? What helps a person to make the leap from paralyzing fear to courage? Relate a time when you felt yourself take that leap.

PERSONAL REFLECTION. The psalmist wrote, "When I am afraid, I will trust in you. . . . In God I trust; I will not be afraid" (Psalm 56:3-4). What are your first thoughts in times of fear or stress? Who do you turn to?

Historically, Esther's courage to go to the king saved a nation. More personally, her courage becomes a model for us. Her circumstances may read like a tale from *The Arabian Nights,* but her decision to risk doing what was right is the kind of decision anyone can make. *Read Esther 5:1-8.*

1. Imagine that you are Esther. What thoughts might you have as you stand in the inner court of the palace?

_____

2. In the face of the king's extravagant offers, why do you think Esther plans one banquet, then another?

_____

3. *Read Esther 7—8.* What approach does Esther use in making her twofold request of the king (7:3-4)?

_____

4. How does Esther dare to be so bold in naming the enemy of the Jews (7:6)?

_____

5. What irony do you see in the fate of Haman and the advance of Mordecai in the king's court?

What biblical principles are underscored by these events?

_____

6. How does the fate of the Jews still hang on Esther's reputation with the king (8:3-6)?

7. When have you gone beyond your own interests to get the privileges you have gained extended to others?

———————————————————————————————————

8. How does the king show his trust in Esther (8:7-8)?

———————————————————————————————————

9. Could you be trusted to be fair with a decree you might write against your enemies? Why or why not?

———————————————————————————————————

10. Every heroic story could be drastically changed by a series of "what if" scenarios. Suggest a "what if" alternative and its consequences for this story.

What can you apply to your own life from the scenario you have chosen?

Ask God to show you the difference you can make for someone else, as well as for yourself, if you trust and obey what he asks you to do.

Now or Later

Read chapters 9—10 to finish the story of Esther. The Days of Purim are still commemorated by the Jewish community. The way in which God worked through Esther is an awesome story to celebrate.

12

The Model Wife

A Portrait of Excellence

Proverbs 31:10-31

Until industrialization, work was not rigidly divided between home and workplace for either men or women. The concept of marriage partnership was taken for granted. Women were often both keepers at home and involved in business ventures to prosper their households. It may have been a patriarchal society, but women were not as confined in their roles as some believe. The previous studies have illustrated that life was far more shoulder-to-shoulder than what became the pattern in the Victorian era.

GROUP DISCUSSION. If you were to write a description of an ideal wife, what would you say?

How many of the traits you have given her reflect who she is as opposed to what she does?

PERSONAL REFLECTION. What makes for a fulfilling life?

This is a discussion of an Old Testament description of an ideal wife. Her life is surprisingly large and satisfying. It will help us take a fresh look at our values. *Read Proverbs 31:10-31.*

1. What is your initial impression of this woman?

2. What qualities are most often mentioned?

3. What responsibilities does this woman have?

What is the sphere of her influence?

4. Think of someone you know today who is like this woman. In what ways are the two alike?

different?

5. What resources does this woman work with?

6. How does the woman's reputation compare with that of her husband?

7. How would you describe this woman's relationship with her husband and family?

8. What is the secret of the woman's praiseworthy life?

———————————————————————————

9. What about this woman's life should become a standard for all women?

Do you think these qualities are limited to women? Why or why not?

———————————————————————————

10. How important is work in making your life meaningful? Explain.

———————————————————————————

11. What is this woman's lasting investment?

What is yours?

Ask God to make your life meaningful in his sight and to give you a sense of purpose—something to aim for in the daily business of everyday life.

Now or Later

At the end of your life, what do you want people to say about you? Record an epitaph that you would like as your memorial.

How do your goals differ from the mainstream view of success?

Leader's Notes

Leading a Bible discussion can be an enjoyable and rewarding experience. But it can also be *scary*—especially if you've never done it before. If this is your feeling, you're in good company. When God asked Moses to lead the Israelites out of Egypt, he replied, "O Lord, please send someone else to do it"! (Ex 4:13). It was the same with Solomon, Jeremiah and Timothy, but God helped these people in spite of their weaknesses, and he will help you as well.

You don't need to be an expert on the Bible or a trained teacher to lead a Bible discussion. The idea behind these inductive studies is that the leader guides group members to discover for themselves what the Bible has to say. This method of learning will allow group members to remember much more of what is said than a lecture would.

These studies are designed to be led easily. As a matter of fact, the flow of questions through the passage from observation to interpretation to application is so natural that you may feel that the studies lead themselves. This study guide is also flexible. You can use it with a variety of groups—student, professional, neighborhood or church groups. Each study takes forty-five to sixty minutes in a group setting.

There are some important facts to know about group dynamics and encouraging discussion. The suggestions listed below should enable you to effectively and enjoyably fulfill your role as leader.

Preparing for the Study

1. Ask God to help you understand and apply the passage in your own life. Unless this happens, you will not be prepared to lead others. Pray too for the various members of the group. Ask God to open your hearts to the message of his Word and motivate you to action.

2. Read the introduction to the entire guide to get an overview of the

entire book and the issues which will be explored.

3. As you begin each study, read and reread the assigned Bible passage to familiarize yourself with it.

4. This study guide is based on the New International Version of the Bible. It will help you and the group if you use this translation as the basis for your study and discussion.

5. Carefully work through each question in the study. Spend time in meditation and reflection as you consider how to respond.

6. Write your thoughts and responses in the space provided in the study guide. This will help you to express your understanding of the passage clearly.

7. It might help to have a Bible dictionary handy. Use it to look up any unfamiliar words, names or places. (For additional help on how to study a passage, see chapter five of *How to Lead a LifeGuide Bible Study*, InterVarsity Press.)

8. Consider how you can apply the Scripture to your life. Remember that the group will follow your lead in responding to the studies. They will not go any deeper than you do.

9. Once you have finished your own study of the passage, familiarize yourself with the leader's notes for the study you are leading. These are designed to help you in several ways. First, they tell you the purpose the study guide author had in mind when writing the study. Take time to think through how the study questions work together to accomplish that purpose. Second, the notes provide you with additional background information or suggestions on group dynamics for various questions. This information can be useful when people have difficulty understanding or answering a question. Third, the leader's notes can alert you to potential problems you may encounter during the study.

10. If you wish to remind yourself of anything mentioned in the leader's notes, make a note to yourself below that question in the study.

Leading the Study

1. Begin the study on time. Open with prayer, asking God to help the group to understand and apply the passage.

2. Be sure that everyone in your group has a study guide. Encourage the group to prepare beforehand for each discussion by reading the introduction to the guide and by working through the questions in the study.

3. At the beginning of your first time together, explain that these studies are meant to be discussions, not lectures. Encourage the members of the group to participate. However, do not put pressure on those who may be hesitant to speak during the first few sessions. You may want to suggest the following guidelines to your group.

■ Stick to the topic being discussed.

■ Your responses should be based on the verses which are the focus of the discussion and not on outside authorities such as commentaries or speakers.

■ These studies focus on a particular passage of Scripture. Only rarely should you refer to other portions of the Bible. This allows for everyone to participate in in-depth study on equal ground.

■ Anything said in the group is considered confidential and will not be discussed outside the group unless specific permission is given to do so.

■ We will listen attentively to each other and provide time for each person present to talk.

■ We will pray for each other.

4. Have a group member read the introduction at the beginning of the discussion.

5. Every session begins with a group discussion question. The question or activity is meant to be used before the passage is read. The question introduces the theme of the study and encourages group members to begin to open up. Encourage as many members as possible to participate, and be ready to get the discussion going with your own response.

This section is designed to reveal where our thoughts or feelings need to be transformed by Scripture. That is why it is especially important not to read the passage before the discussion question is asked. The passage will tend to color the honest reactions people would otherwise give because they are, of course, supposed to think the way the Bible does.

You may want to supplement the group discussion question with an icebreaker to help people to get comfortable. See the community section of *Small Group Idea Book* for more ideas.

You also might want to use the personal reflection question with your group. Either allow a time of silence for people to respond individually or discuss it together.

6. Have a group member (or members if the passage is long) read

aloud the passage to be studied. Then give people several minutes to read the passage again silently so that they can take it all in.

7. Question 1 will generally be an overview question designed to briefly survey the passage. Encourage the group to look at the whole passage, but try to avoid getting sidetracked by questions or issues that will be addressed later in the study.

8. As you ask the questions, keep in mind that they are designed to be used just as they are written. You may simply read them aloud. Or you may prefer to express them in your own words.

There may be times when it is appropriate to deviate from the study guide. For example, a question may have already been answered. If so, move on to the next question. Or someone may raise an important question not covered in the guide. Take time to discuss it, but try to keep the group from going off on tangents.

9. Avoid answering your own questions. If necessary, repeat or rephrase them until they are clearly understood. Or point out something you read in the leader's notes to clarify the context or meaning. An eager group quickly becomes passive and silent if they think the leader will do most of the talking.

10. Don't be afraid of silence. People may need time to think about the question before formulating their answers.

11. Don't be content with just one answer. Ask, "What do the rest of you think?" or "Anything else?" until several people have given answers to the question.

12. Acknowledge all contributions. Try to be affirming whenever possible. Never reject an answer. If it is clearly off-base, ask, "Which verse led you to that conclusion?" or again, "What do the rest of you think?"

13. Don't expect every answer to be addressed to you, even though this will probably happen at first. As group members become more at ease, they will begin to truly interact with each other. This is one sign of healthy discussion.

14. Don't be afraid of controversy. It can be very stimulating. If you don't resolve an issue completely, don't be frustrated. Move on and keep it in mind for later. A subsequent study may solve the problem.

15. Periodically summarize what the group has said about the passage. This helps to draw together the various ideas mentioned and gives continuity to the study. But don't preach.

16. At the end of the Bible discussion you may want to allow group members a time of quiet to work on an idea under "Now or Later." Then discuss what you experienced. Or you may want to encourage group members to work on these ideas between meetings. Give an opportunity during the session for people to talk about what they are learning.

17. Conclude your time together with conversational prayer, adapting the prayer suggestion at the end of the study to your group. Ask for God's help in following through on the commitments you've made.

18. End on time.

Many more suggestions and helps are found in *How to Lead a LifeGuide Bible Study*, which is part of the LifeGuide Bible Study series.

Components of Small Groups

A healthy small group should do more than study the Bible. There are four components to consider as you structure your time together.

Nurture. Small groups help us to grow in our knowledge and love of God. Bible study is the key to making this happen and is the foundation of your small group.

Community. Small groups are a great place to develop deep friendships with other Christians. Allow time for informal interaction before and after each study. Plan activities and games that will help you get to know each other. Spend time having fun together—going on a picnic or cooking dinner together.

Worship and prayer. Your study will be enhanced by spending time praising God together in prayer or song. Pray for each other's needs—and keep track of how God is answering prayer in your group. Ask God to help you to apply what you are learning in your study.

Outreach. Reaching out to others can be a practical way of applying what you are learning, and it will keep your group from becoming self-focused. Host a series of evangelistic discussions for your friends or neighbors. Clean up the yard of an elderly friend. Serve at a soup kitchen together, or spend a day working on a Habitat house.

Many more suggestions and helps in each of these areas are found in *Small Group Idea Book*. Information on building a small group can be found in *Small Group Leaders' Handbook* and *The Big Book on Small Groups* (both from InterVarsity Press). Reading through one of these books would be worth your time.

Study 1. The First Woman: A Far-Reaching Choice. Genesis 3:1-13.

Purpose: To understand the far-reaching effects of our choices.

Group discussion. Be prepared to reveal something from your own life when this question is discussed. Everyone has been tempted, so even if this question seems too revealing, it will apply to everyone. The goal of the question is to get the group to see how clever the Tempter is and how he exploits our weak spots. We can all relate to what happened with the first woman and understand in a fresh way why this is called "the Fall."

Question 1. Male and female in the image of God in a garden prepared by the Creator with every kind of tree for food—this is the environment in which the events of chapter 3 take place. God is present. He has involved himself in the lives of these two persons and provided everything they need.

Question 2. The serpent begins a theological conversation. God is the subject. "Has God said" becomes an opportunity for the serpent to plant seeds of doubt as to whether God really meant what he said and whether he might be cheating the woman out of some good thing.

Question 3. Sometimes we extend God's commands to keep from making mistakes. The woman and the man may have discussed God's instruction and decided to avoid the tree as much as possible—not necessarily a bad idea. But we make these rules only for ourselves. When we make them for others we sponsor a meaningless legalism. Rules do not make people holy; choices do.

Question 4. Notice the fruit of the tree has three enticing descriptions in verse 6. It is best not to stand around contemplating what is forbidden. No wonder Paul told Timothy to "flee the evil desires of youth" (2 Tim 2:22). Perhaps the serpent made his initial approach to the woman because of her aesthetic sensibilities.

Questions 5-6. The idea that she might become like God seemed a good thing. Why remain innocent if they could be like God? Wouldn't fellowship with him be even better if they were on his level? These may have been the woman's thoughts. (She is not called Eve until 3:20.) Her focus was on her fulfillment—not on what God had said.

Question 8. The man and his wife hide from the One who made them. Sin always makes people hide. They know shame for the first time. Shame is the feeling that things are not what they should be. The man and woman turn on each other. Fellowship is broken on both the vertical and the horizontal levels.

Question 9. God's grace is evident in that he comes to find them. Doesn't he know where they are when he calls, "Where are you?" Yes, but the man and woman need to know where they are. He gives them opportunity to look at what they had done. A look ahead to verse 15 shows that God already has a plan to crush the serpent through a woman's offspring—the first promise of a Savior.

Question 10. Decisions that seem small to us often have long-range impact on our lives. Sometimes we are blind to the importance of our choices. God's Word teaches us how to think, how to evaluate what is important. It is our guide for living.

Study 2. Sarah & Hagar: Waiting for God to Act. Genesis 16; 18:1-15.

Purpose: To learn the importance of waiting for God to act.

Question 1. In her culture Sarai would assume that she had no children because of some inadequacy on her part. From time to time God reminds Sarai and Abram that their progeny will make a great nation, but Sarai does not produce any babies. Failure is all she knows. She must have felt keenly the humiliation of infertility.

Question 2. Sarai may have thought that God didn't mean that it would be her baby. Abram was getting older and so was she. She couldn't wait any longer; if God couldn't do it, she would do it herself!

Question 3. It was Sarai's idea to use a surrogate mother, but she found it easy to blame Abram. After all, he didn't stand up against the idea. Taking matters into her own hands had not produced the blessing she was looking for.

Question 4. The Lord intervenes for Hagar; he hears, and he gives her a promise. She says that she has seen the Lord and lived to tell about it (v. 13). He tells her the baby will be a boy, gives him a name and tells what his disposition will be. God knows about this event that troubles her so much. Hagar may well have been one of the maidservants that Pharoah, king of Egypt, gave to Abraham in Genesis 12:16, a sordid story in itself.

Question 5. Going back to Sarai meant eating humble pie. It meant doing what Sarai said and taking all her disdain without complaint. However, the child would be born in the household of his father.

Question 6. Three men came to the middle of nowhere to seek out Abraham and his wife, Sarah. They wanted to talk over two things with Abraham: the promised son and the destruction of Sodom. One of these men turns out to be the Lord (this is called a *theophany*: God in the appearance of a man). The men go through all of the hospitality rituals of the culture that set the stage for conversation about important matters. Their visit is meant for Sarah as well as Abraham. They ask for his wife and in her hearing give the promise again. Sarah's laughter may have been her way of guarding herself against the disappointment she felt previously when her prayers weren't answered.

Question 7. God knows Sarah's name, her secret thoughts and her fears. Sarah did not know that this knowledge was safe with the Lord.

Question 9. Genesis 21:1-7 answers the question the Lord asks in 18:14, "Is anything too hard for the LORD?" The words "Is anything too hard for God?" were spoken in another form to Mary when she learned that she would bear a son and that Elizabeth was also with child. Sarah had to learn not only about God's power but also what it meant to wait for his timing. The Lord would return at the appointed time and Sarah would have a son, despite her unbelief.

Study 3. Miriam: A Critical Spirit. Numbers 12.

Purpose: To learn about the danger of criticizing others.

Group discussion. Very often personal uncertainty lies behind a critical spirit. Someone threatens our role or what we think or how we feel about ourselves. We need to learn to distinguish between valid insights and a critical spirit.

Question 1. Their complaint about Moses' Cushite wife was only a pretext for their complaint about the exclusive nature of Moses' prophetic gift. Did God only speak through Moses?

Question 2. Miriam and Aaron imply that Moses has an arrogant attitude about his leadership—that God only speaks through him. God's view of Moses is that he is a faithful, humble servant, and that God has a special relationship with him. He speaks to Moses as a friend.

Question 3. Micah 6:4 tells us that both Miriam and Aaron had positions of leadership along with Moses. Miriam's cleverness in suggesting that she find a Hebrew nurse for the baby Moses when Pharaoh's daughter found him in the river is evidence that she had good leadership qualities even as a young girl. Her influence on the people is also felt at the time of the exodus. She is called a prophetess and leads the singing of a song she composed—a song the children of Israel sang for generations following the exodus, found in Exodus 15:20-21. Probably Moses, Aaron and Miriam led the people as a triumvirate.

Question 6. The Lord hears their complaints; he acts promptly (at once); he comes down to confront the leadership team; he speaks of Moses with affection and affirmation; he punishes.

Question 7. God summoned all three of them because Moses needed affirmation; he needed to know God's point of view.

Question 9. Be prepared for questions about God discriminating against women. Could it be that Miriam was the spokesperson for the complaint? Are women often more verbal about relational difficulties? Aaron is the priest in the service of the Tabernacle. He is also quick to call his action sin. Maybe Miriam bears the punishment for both of them. Is Aaron really exempt from the anger of the Lord? You won't be able to answer all of these questions, but in asking them and other questions you can encourage the group to see that discrimination may not be the best answer.

Question 12. This question points back to the group discussion question about discernment versus criticism. Draw on what you have learned from the study.

Study 4. Rahab: An Unlikely Ally. Joshua 2; 6:15-25.

Purpose: To witness the courage of personal faith.

Question 1. Josephus and other early sources refer to Rahab as an "innkeeper." That would account for the men seeking lodging at her house. It would also make her house the place where their presence would cause the least suspicion.

Question 3. Expect the group to give you strong impressions from what is written in the text about Rahab, using a bit of imagination about the forceful and purposeful ways she acted to protect the men. She probably had many reasons for making a deal with the spies, but her actions demonstrated clearly whose side she was on. This is a woman who has chosen to be on God's side and takes the risk. Some of your group may mention that she is rewarded for lying. Don't let this become a lengthy discussion; this pagan woman had many needs. She needed to learn about both lying and prostitution, and probably many other things. It was not her lie that saved the men; it was her choosing to help them.

Question 5. Rahab's confession to these men has an interesting structure.

She begins with "I know" and ends with "The LORD your God is God." In between she says "we have heard." She has accurate information about what God has done for his people. Notice particularly the verbs in verses 8-11.

Question 6. Rahab later showed her faith by gathering her whole family into her house and by placing the scarlet cord in the window as soon as the spies told her to do so. The scarlet cord is similar to the blood of the Passover Lamb on the doorpost in Exodus 12:13, 22-23.

Question 7. Joshua chose two men who had spied out the land, who would know about Rahab, and sent them to her house where she had gathered her family in hiding, dependent on that scarlet cord to save her from the fate of the city. Rahab had asked for an assurance when she let the men down the wall with a rope at the time she saved their lives. They promised her they would "treat [her] kindly and faithfully when the LORD gives us the land" (Josh 2:14). They made it clear that deliverance of the city was the Lord's business, and she staked her confidence on that hope.

Question 9. Rahab is listed in the genealogy of Jesus. Four women are mentioned in Matthew's telescoped list, an unusual practice in Jewish genealogies. Rahab's inclusion indicates God's grace and concern for Gentiles.

Questions 10-11. Encourage group members to be specific. Our decisions are full of cause and effect. Help the group see that ordinary people trusting God can accomplish his purposes. Rahab was a nobody; her obedience put her in the list of biblical heroes.

Study 5. Ruth: The Cost of Loyalty. Ruth 1—2.

Purpose: To understand the cost and value of loyalty.

Group Discussion. Loyalty is becoming a rare virtue. "I'll go with you unless someone better comes along" seems a popular way to act. This question should lead to discussion about the cost of loyalty and what a lack of loyalty reveals about our character.

Question 1. As a matter of interest, the Moabites are descendants of Lot's oldest daughter who, though rescued from the destruction of Sodom and Gomorrah, chose to live apart from God's people (see Gen 19:37). Ruth's choices are in sharp contrast to this. Through all the famine, the refugee status that pained the family, the hand of God brings Ruth into a marriage that may even have been frowned on by her own people.

Question 3. Ruth leaves the familiar, choosing to identify with the true God and his people. In contrast, Orpah returns to her people and to her gods (1:15), choosing what is familiar.

Questions 4-5. Ruth's choice is much like the decision to become a Christian, particularly if a person comes from a non-Christian family. She casts her lot with the people of God and turns her back on the past.

Question 6. Don't minimize the significance of this question. Diligence and dependability in the workplace are an important part of our witness. The favorable comment of the harvesters is part of Ruth's reputation in the community.

Question 7. Boaz has heard of Ruth's loyalty to her mother-in-law. He is sensitive to all it cost Ruth to come back with Naomi (2:11). He sees Ruth in the protection of the God of Israel. In contrast, Ruth sees herself as a foreigner, having a standing lower than the servants of Boaz (2:10, 13).

Question 9. This is a question about values. What is worth giving yourself to? Ask how one demonstrates loyalty to another person.

Study 6. Naomi: Sadness Swallowed Up by Joy. Ruth 3—4.

Purpose: To show God's faithful care for those who trust him.

Question 1. It's easy to read of Naomi's losses in a few sentences and miss the reality of the pain she must have experienced. Use your imagination to appreciate some of her bereft feelings. The meaning of names was important in Hebrew culture. Naomi felt her name (Pleasant) no longer matched the realities of her life.

Question 2. "The kinsman-redeemer was responsible for protecting the interests of needy members of the extended family—e.g., to provide an heir for a brother who had died (Deut 25:5-10), to redeem land that a poor relative had sold outside the family (Lev 25:25-28), to redeem a relative who had been sold into slavery (Lev 25:47-49) and to avenge the killing of a relative (Num 35:19-21)" (*NIV Study Bible* [Grand Rapids, Mich.: Zondervan, 1985], p. 367).

A ray of hope entered Naomi's mind when she first heard that Ruth had been gleaning in the fields of Boaz. If Boaz would be a kinsman-redeemer for them, their economic and social problems would be solved. If he refused, both women would feel disgraced, and Ruth would lose her place for winnowing.

Question 3. In the Hebrew economy the land and the family name were linked. Naomi had no male heir for the land that belonged to her husband and her sons. Her plan was to have Boaz, a kinsman-redeemer, rescue her and Ruth from this plight.

Question 4. Boaz is a man of integrity. He summons the kinsman first in line before the elders of the people to find out if he wishes to redeem the land Naomi has offered. The kinsman is willing until he finds out it includes marriage to Ruth. He already has an heir, so he refuses. Boaz addresses Ruth as "my daughter," which may indicate a difference in age. It may also account for Boaz's pleasure that one as young and attractive as Ruth would ask for his protection (3:10).

Question 6. Boaz gives Naomi a future by becoming her kinsman-redeemer. Her family line is established; she receives the possibility of an heir and care for the future. The birth of Obed is as if Naomi had given birth to a son, because she now has an heir.

Question 7. This question may have several answers. Certainly the birth of hope is the core of the change in her life. She saw no possibilities when she returned; she seems to have forgotten that Boaz was a possible means of rescue. When she sees God's hand in leading Ruth to glean in Boaz's fields, things began to change in Naomi's eyes.

Question 8. To claim Jesus as our kinsman-redeemer is not a far-fetched idea. The symbolism of the gospel carries the idea that Jesus spreads his garment of salvation over us and restores us to our rightful place and gives us our inheritance. The prophet Isaiah spoke of being covered with garments of salvation (Is 61:10) much like Boaz spreading his garment over Ruth that brought her a whole new life.

Question 9. Ruth, along with Rahab, has a place in the genealogy of Jesus Christ, even though she was a Gentile. Jesus came for prostitutes and for Gentiles; it is appropriate, therefore, that both have a place in the genealogy. Ruth chose to identify with the people of God and go with Naomi even though she returned empty to her own people. Their simple obedience and faith brought about the birth of an important ancestor in the kingly line—something Naomi never dreamed of.

Study 7. Hannah: From Misery to Praise. 1 Samuel 1:1—2:11.

Purpose: To show that God's gracious answer to our pain is himself.

Question 1. Hannah was not only barren in a culture where a woman's sense of worth depended on childbearing, but she had an antagonist in the second wife. (Perhaps the second wife was taken in response to her barrenness.) Further, annual religious rites at Shiloh regularly reminded her of this pain. It seemed as if God didn't care.

Question 2. Hannah, weeping and without appetite for food, goes before the Lord. He is the LORD Almighty. This is the first time in the Bible this name (the LORD of Hosts) is used for God. Is anything too hard for him? Though he is the LORD, transcendent and powerful, he is also near. She asks him to *look,* to *remember,* to *not forget,* to *give* to her. She prays, feels assured and expects an answer. Then she eats contentedly.

Question 3. If people in your group do not respond with personal examples, ask: "What are some ways people in our culture soothe their hurts?" Alcohol, drugs, medicines, sex, career fixation and so on.

Question 4. Don't let this question be answered superficially. Pain reveals more about our character and beliefs than we sometimes want to admit.

Question 5. Levites traditionally served from ages twenty-five to fifty. Other vows were taken for a more limited time. Hannah gives Samuel to the Lord for his whole life. (Children in the East were usually nursed for a minimum of three years, often longer.)

Question 6. Chapter one focuses on a child; chapter two focuses on God.

Question 7. If possible, as group members find them, list Hannah's beliefs on a board or pad of paper. It will make the next question easier.

Question 9. Hannah's joy is in God, not her son. The real solution to pain is for God to show us himself. She worships and gives thanks for who he is.

Study 8. Abigail: A Level-Headed Woman. 1 Samuel 25:2-44.

Purpose: To see the effects of wisdom and courage in crisis situations.

Question 1. David's situation is described in 1 Samuel 23:13-14. Nabal is a rich farmer who is a fool. His servants have better judgment in personal relationships than he does. Obviously, Abigail has a difficult marriage.

Questions 2-3. David had been in Nabal's area with six hundred men who guarded Nabal's shepherds and flocks from marauders. The servants give evidence that these six hundred never took what they wanted. David now asks to share in the festival. (Sheep shearing was a festive occasion.)

Question 4. This was probably not the first time the servants had gone to Abigail. They recognized her as a resourceful, intelligent woman.

Question 5. Abigail was a beautiful woman, going alone into a camp of six hundred angry men. She must have rehearsed her speech on the way many times. She was willing to take the blame for Nabal's action (though she defines him accurately) to appease David and get him to listen to her.

Question 7. Abigail is aware that David is God's man. She knows he has lived with honor, not taking vengeance into his own hands. (David must have been a legend in the area.) She reminds him of who he is in the Lord's sight and what the Lord's purpose is for him.

Question 9. Abigail rescued Nabal—or tried to. She rescued the servants and herself and, perhaps of greater importance, she rescued David from acting in anger and haste.

Study 9. The Shunammite Woman: Taking the Initiative. 2 Kings 4:8-37.
Purpose: To show how the initiative to do good leads to greater faith.

Question 1. This unnamed woman is well-to-do, evidently has a big house, and her husband is a successful farmer. She also has independence to act and to take initiative, to command servants and to travel alone—abilities not usually associated with women of this era.

Question 2. The woman recognized that Elisha was a prophet of God. Evidently she was eager to have him minister in her area, bringing the word of the Lord. Her generosity meant comfort for Elisha, a home environment and provision for his practical needs.

Question 4. The woman had doubtless borne much personal sorrow over her childlessness. Her husband was old, the family name would die out, and she would have little support and comfort in her old age. Could she dare to believe that God could and would give her a child? Trusting that Elisha could do something about her need did not come easily. It is sometimes easier to give than to receive.

Question 5. The woman lays the boy in Elisha's room, thus keeping the household from knowledge of his death. She sets out to find Elisha and will not be deterred by anyone else. She doesn't even want to discuss it with anyone but Elisha.

Question 8. The woman's strong resolve is to get Elisha to act for her. She feels that he must do something because he is responsible for her having this son in the first place. She had hardly dared to hope that she would be a mother. She does not go with Gehazi but clings to Elisha. He must come and restore her son. Her faith in him will not let him go. It is an example of persistent, believing prayer.

Her other options were to wail in the village, to seek sympathy and support from the community. Or she could have cursed God for this sickness or blamed her husband for not taking better care of the boy. She chose instead to find the one person who had power to do something about it.

Summarize this study carefully, reviewing the lessons learned from the Shunammite woman's life.

Study 10. Esther: Captive in a Strange Land. Esther 2—4.

Purpose: To show how character rises above circumstances.

Questions 1-2. Esther was not responsible for the death of her parents, her nationality, her beauty, her exile or being chosen for the king's harem. She seemed to have little control over what was happening to her. Yet she could control how she acted in those circumstances. It is obvious that she did not make her situation more difficult by rebelling or being bitter.

Question 4. Chapter 2:12-14 shows the inhumanity of polygamy. The women in a harem were more likely to live as widows than as married women. Though each woman went before the king, there was no guarantee that the king would even remember her name or call for her again. She would never have a home of her own. The emotional deprivation of never really belonging to a person whom you loved would be very great.

Question 5. Mordecai demonstrates fatherly care for Esther, which allowed her to trust him. She repeatedly does what he says, which indicates respect and love on her part. The advice he gives her shows wisdom. He goes out of his way to keep in touch with her, always through intermediaries. He is faithful to the king under whom he serves and gets messages to Esther which save the king's life. He is also a man of conscience. He refuses to compromise by bowing down to Haman.

Question 6. Mordecai goes into the open square in front of the king's gate, wailing loudly and bitterly. This also gets him in touch with Esther. Jews everywhere made similar public protests. They went to the streets with their complaints. In 3:15 there is evidence that the citizenry was bewildered by the edict and protested.

Question 7. Mordecai does not see life as a collection of incidents or mishaps but believes that he, Esther and the nation are in the hands of an unseen guide.

Question 8. He gives Esther three arguments: (1) Esther herself is not exempt from the edict; (2) God will not permit his people to be destroyed. If Esther fails, help will come another way, but Esther and her family will be losers; (3) she may have come to her present position for just such a time as this.

Questions 9-10. Esther wants the community of Jews to be involved in what she does. She needs their support. The fasting would bind the people together and, although no mention is made of prayer, Old Testament fasting involved repentance and prayer. Esther needs God's help for courage. The people need clean hearts. She needs God's blessing. The nation needs deliverance. A sense of loyalty and honor, of personal integrity, are essential for Esther to do what is clearly her duty.

Study 11. Esther: Courage to Act. Esther 5:1-8; 7—8.

Purpose: To see a demonstration of courage.

Group Discussion. Courage is not something you store up; it comes from a reservoir of smaller right actions made daily in life. It is closely related to your life view. Do you save your life or lose it for something bigger than yourself?

Question 1. Think of how carefully Esther dressed and perfumed herself. She must have gone over every detail and possible option in her mind repeatedly before leaving her room. She needed confidence that she was part of a larger plan, sovereignly controlled by God. Joyce Baldwin in her Tyndale Commentary on Esther remarks, "The dramatic tension between human relationships and the overriding demands of royal protocol is always full of fascination" (*Esther,* Tyndale Old Testament Commentary [Downers Grove, Ill.: InterVarsity Press, 1984], p. 86).

Question 2. Esther's plan is to see if the king will receive her and accept her approach with favor. She already has the banquet prepared. Esther's request seems an anticlimax to her bravery in initiating contact with the king. Baldwin points out that it was not in keeping with protocol for the queen to disclose her mind at a formal occasion in the throne room. She needed a much less public dinner party. It was a daring move to invite Haman as the only guest.

Question 3. The story allows responses to come slowly—in the Eastern way. Let the king mellow in this attention. Let his curiosity pique. Surely Esther took this bold move with something significant in mind, the king muses. Notice Esther's deferential words which remind the king that she is the queen and important to him: "If the king regards me with favor and if it pleases the king to grant my petition" (5:8).

The king, mellowed by food and wine and attention from the queen, reclines on his couch and asks the question that has beguiled him. What does she want? It could not have occurred to him that Esther's request would be for her life. He was thinking *things;* she was thinking *life.*

Esther chose a startling way to reveal her nationality. Once Esther sets the stage with her deferential "if" clauses, she socks it to him.

Question 4. Esther was interrupted by the king. She had given no reference to Haman until the king asked who would have the audacity to threaten the queen's life. Haman himself was probably relaxed and glowing in this privileged company, since these honors meant so much to him. He was terrified to learn who Esther was, but he could not escape, and the king acted swiftly.

Question 5. Haman is hung on the very gallows he prepared for Mordecai. The principles: "God opposes the proud but gives grace to the humble" (Jas 4:6). "A man reaps what he sows" (Gal 6:7). "Do to others what you would have them do to you" (Mt 7:12), and so on.

Question 6. Esther was given Haman's estate. Mordecai was given Haman's honored position. The king was concerned about the two of them. But the matter of the Jewish nation was still not solved. If Esther had stopped at that point, accepting only personal deliverance, she would have sacrificed the larger community of Jews.

Note how the order of Esther's "if" clauses change in this appeal to the king (8:5). Look at all the phrases that reveal her pain over her people.

Question 8. This king got in trouble before because he didn't worry about the details and gave authority to the wrong people. His recent understanding of Mordecai's heroism (which saved the king) and his concern for Esther must have given him some confidence that he could trust them. Power in the hands of people with impure motives is a dangerous thing. How do you use the power you have?

Study 12. The Model Wife: A Portrait of Excellence. Proverbs 31:10-31.
Purpose: To explore the relevance of this ideal standard for us.
Questions 1-2. This woman is a hard worker. She is a provider. Notice the verbs that tell of her activity.

Question 3. She is a community figure. She is known in the business world of her day as well as at home. She is a smart manager in both realms.

Question 5. She has money to trade. She has money to invest. She is an Old Testament entrepreneur. Yet she is also a woman of compassion. Notice the strong imagery of verse 20 that tells of her relationship with the needy.

Question 6. Is being respected at the city gate among the elders more valuable than the respect and praise this woman gets for what she does? Verse 31 indicates she is praised at the city gate too. She is known for wisdom and faithful instruction.

Question 8. Her praiseworthy life is not based on charm and beauty, both of which, though attractive, are temporary. She fears the Lord and lives her life before him.

Questions 10. Work is a gift from God. It has its own rewards. We need a renewed theology of work. This woman found satisfaction in being productive. People who think they have no contribution to make often struggle with low self-esteem and dissatisfaction. The strength of this woman's life is seen in what she produces. Her works praise her. Like a circle, work can produce character and character produces a willingness to work.

Question 11. This woman's lasting investment is the fear of the Lord. She has done her work under his view. His standards matter to her. What would we change in the way we invest our time (energy) if we were to properly fear the Lord? What she has accomplished by her industry is not for the sake of personal greed but for others who rise up and call her blessed.

Gladys Hunt is a freelance writer living in Grand Rapids, Michigan. She and her husband, Keith, worked with InterVarsity students for many years. She is the author of some twenty books and numerous Fisherman Bible study guides published by Waterbrook Press, including The God Who Understands Me, Hebrews, John, Luke, Relationships, Revelation *and* Romans. *She is also the author of the books* Honey for a Child's Heart, Honey for a Woman's Heart *and* Honey for a Teenager's Heart *(Zondervan) and coauthor of* For Christ and the University *(IVP).*

What Should We Study Next?

A good place to continue your study of Scripture would be with a book study. Many groups begin with a Gospel such as *Mark* (20 studies by Jim Hoover) or *John* (26 studies by Douglas Connelly). These guides are divided into two parts so that if twenty or twenty-six weeks seems like too much to do at once, the group can feel free to do half and take a break with another topic. Later you might want to come back to it. You might prefer to try a shorter letter. *Philippians* (9 studies by Donald Baker), *Ephesians* (11 studies by Andrew T. and Phyllis J. Le Peau) and *1 & 2 Timothy and Titus* (11 studies by Pete Sommer) are good options. If you want to vary your reading with an Old Testament book, consider *Ecclesiastes* (12 studies by Bill and Teresa Syrios) for a challenging and exciting study.

There are a number of interesting topical LifeGuide studies as well. Here are some options for filling three or four quarters of a year:

Basic Discipleship
Christian Beliefs, 12 studies by Stephen D. Eyre
Christian Character, 12 studies by Andrea Sterk & Peter Scazzero
Christian Disciplines, 12 studies by Andrea Sterk & Peter Scazzero
Evangelism, 12 studies by Rebecca Pippert & Ruth Siemens

Building Community
Christian Community, 10 studies by Rob Suggs
Fruit of the Spirit, 9 studies by Hazel Offner
Spiritual Gifts, 12 studies by Charles & Anne Hummel

Character Studies
David, 12 studies by Jack Kuhatschek
New Testament Characters, 12 studies by Carolyn Nystrom
Old Testament Characters, 12 studies by Peter Scazzero

The Trinity
Meeting God, 12 studies by J. I. Packer
Meeting Jesus, 13 studies by Leighton Ford
Meeting the Spirit, 12 studies by Douglas Connelly